My Little Prayer Book

June Eaton

Jeannie Harmon

Ellen F. Pill

Publications International, Ltd.

June Eaton is a freelance writer and former teacher whose published work includes Sunday school curriculums as well as stories and articles in more than 50 Christian publications. She has also contributed to many books, including *The Bible: A to Z*, *This Too Shall Pass*, and *A Mother's Daily Prayer Book*.

Jeannie Harmon is a freelance writer who has written a number of children's religious books including *Peter Follows Jesus*, *My Jesus Pocket Book: Prayer*, and *David and the Giant*. In addition, many of her articles have appeared in publications such as *Happy Acres: Creative Children's Church Curriculum*, *Quiet Hour*, and *The Vision*.

Ellen F. Pill is a writer who has contributed to several inspirational books, including *Blessed by an Angel* and *Echoes of Love: Baby*. In addition, her stories and sentiments have been published in *Whispers from Heaven* magazine as well as by American Greetings and Hallmark.

Cover: Artville

Illustrations: Joyce Shelton, Denise Hilton Campbell, Jody Wheeler

Scriptures quoted from the *International Children's Bible®, New Century Version®*, copyright © 1986, 1988, 1999 by Tommy Nelson®, a division of Thomas Nelson, Inc. Nashville, Tennessee 37214. Used by permission.

Louis Weber, CEO
Publications International, Ltd.
7373 North Cicero Avenue
Lincolnwood, Illinois 60712

Manufactured in China.

8 7 6 5 4 3 2 1

ISBN-13: 978-1-60553-972-0
ISBN-10: 1-60553-972-4

Library of Congress Control Number: 2010926311

Contents

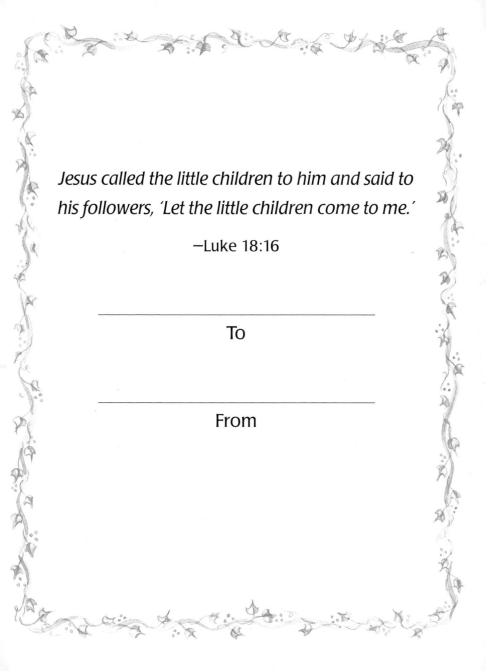

Jesus called the little children to him and said to his followers, 'Let the little children come to me.'

—Luke 18:16

_____

To

_____

From

Chapter One

Rise and Shine

Have you ever wondered who God is?
Our God, who lives in heaven, made
the sun and all the wonderful things
we see. He makes everything work
together to help us live and grow so
well—the sunlight and the plants, the
rain and the earth, the animals and
human beings.

God is a loving God: He knows how to
make a beautiful world! Our prayers
to him can help us say "Thank you for
such a wonderful gift!"

It is good to praise the Lord....
It is good to tell of your love in the morning
and of your loyalty at night.

—Psalm 92:1, 2

The Lord's Prayer

Our Father in heaven,
we pray that your name will
    always be kept holy.
We pray that your kingdom
    will come.
We pray that what you want
    will be done,
here on earth as it is in heaven.
Give us the food we need for
    each day.
Forgive the sins we have done,
just as we have forgiven those who did
    wrong to us.
Do not cause us to be tested;
but save us from the evil one.

Morning Song

I open my eyes
    and what do I see?
I see your world smiling—
    It's smiling at me!

I listen so hard
    and what do I hear?
A sweet morning song
    playing right in my ear!

I feel with my heart
    and what do I know?
There are many people
    who love me so!

It's Me, God!

Hi, God!

It's me.

I just wanted to say "Good Morning,"

And I hope you have a good day.

Amen.

Happy Sun

Good-bye to the moon,

Hello, happy sun!

I have a feeling

Today will be fun!

A Brand-New Day

Dear God, I know you made this brand-new day just for me. I want it to be great! Please show me how to be helpful and kind at school and at home. I want you to be proud of me.

Sunny Day

Good morning, God! The sun is a bright, warm smile coming in my window. I want to jump out of bed and sing. I wonder what the day will bring? Today I'm ready for anything! Thank you, God, for the sun.

Good Morning, Dear Lord Jesus

Good morning, dear Lord Jesus,
It's time to start the day.
Be with me every moment
As I walk along the way.

Keep me safe in your arms
And guide my steps, I pray,
Pick me up when I fall down
And never let me stray.

Amen.

Sunshine in My Soul

There is sunshine in my soul today,
More glorious and bright
Than glows in any earthly sky,
For Jesus is my light.

Oh, there's sunshine, blessed sunshine,
   While the peaceful, happy moments
   roll;
When Jesus shows His smiling face,
   There is sunshine in my soul.

There is gladness in my soul today,
   And hope, and peace, and love,
For blessing which He gives me now,
   For joy laid up above.

Oh, there's sunshine, blessed sunshine,
   While the peaceful, happy moments
   roll;
When Jesus shows His smiling face,
   There is sunshine in my soul.

—Eliza Hewitt

Going to Church

Good morning, God. It's Sunday, and I'm coming to your house today. I love to go to church! The music makes me think of angels singing, and I like to hear the words from the Bible. They help me feel close to you. Whenever I'm in church, I know you're there, too. I can't wait to be with you today!

What Do You Do
in the Morning, God?

What do you do in the morning, God?
I get up and wash my face and brush my
teeth. I take off my pajamas and put on play
clothes or get ready for school.

Then Mom sets out my favorite cereal for
breakfast. I like to hear the *crunch, crunch,
crunch* as I'm chewing, and I like the way my
tummy feels so nice
and full when I'm
done. Is that
what you do,
too, God?

Lord Teach Us

By the prayers of Jesus, Lord teach us
how to pray.

By the gifts of Jesus, Lord teach us how
to give.

By the toils of Jesus, Lord teach us how
to work.

By the love of Jesus,
Lord teach us how
to love.

By the cross of Jesus,
Lord teach us
how to live.

For God loved the world so much that he gave his only Son. God gave his Son so that whoever believes in him may not be lost, but have eternal life.

—John 3:16

Your Love Is
Like the Sunshine

Thank you for the morning sun
That through my window shines,
Reminding me of the great love
You have for humankind.

For little children everywhere,
Each day starts just the same—
Your loving arms reach down to us.
You call us each by name.

You whisper we're your children
And you're our loving dad,
Providing all the things we need
To make our hearts so glad.

The morning's always better
When we know that you are here.
You fill our hearts with gladness
And start our days with cheer.

Thank You for the Morning

Get up, little birdie!
Get up, big, bright sun!
Get up, trees and flowers,
It's time to have some fun.

Get up, little puppy,
So sleepy in your bed.
Let's run and play for hours,
Don't lie in bed instead!

Thanks, God, for the morning
When all is clear and bright.
Thank you, God, for playtime.
It makes my world all right!

What Am I Going to Do?

What am I going to do today?
I really have no clue.
But I know that you'll be with me
in anything I do.

God, please lend your help
if I need a guiding light.
Keep me safe through all the day
'til it's time to say good night.

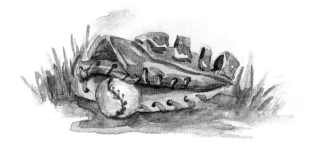

Help Me Today

My God,
    I know you're watching
    as this new day starts.
Dear God,
    I know you're with me—
    I keep you in my heart.

Today, it won't be easy,
I'm feeling very sad.
But I know when you're beside me,
Nothing seems so bad.

So God,
    Please stay close
    as we go hand in hand—
And God,
    I'll try to always think of you
    and learn to understand.

Hello, Sun!

I love to see the sunshine in the morning, Lord. It lets me know you're with me. It reminds me to smile and say, "Thank you!" as I begin another new day!

Animals in the Zoo

We're going to the zoo today. I love it there! I wonder if the polar bears will be swimming in their pool? Or if the elephants will spray each other with their trunks? I love all animals, Lord. Thank you for making them. Please keep them safe and care for them.

A Noisy Night

Thunder woke me last night, God. The noise was so loud and scary it made me jump. I hid under my blanket and covered my ears.

I don't like to be afraid, Lord. Next time the thunder comes, please keep my heart from pounding so hard. Be with me so I'll stay calm. (And thank you for giving me this nice, quiet morning to wake up to.)

I'm Glad It's Morning

I'm glad it's morning, God.
It's sunny and so bright.
The sun's rays chase the fears away
That I had throughout the night.

I don't know why I'm fearful
When I know you're by my side.
I just get scared and tremble
And really want to hide.

Lord, thank you for the morning
To chase my fears away.
Giving me a happy heart
To have throughout the day.

Rainy Day

The sky this morning is as dark as night,
God, and my window is sprinkled with
raindrops that look like tears. The whole
world seems sad. Help me not to feel sad,
too, Lord. You made rainy days as well as
sunny ones. Everything you make is good.
Show me the good things about a rainy day,
even if I can't go out to play.

I Don't Want to Get Up, God

Lord, I'm feeling sad today. I don't even want to get out of bed. Can I stay here and talk to you? I know I'd feel better if I told you what was bothering me. You always understand. Thanks, God. I love that I can tell you anything that's bothering me. Amen.

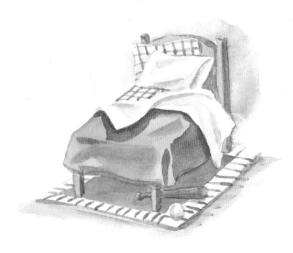

A New Day

This is a new day,
a brand-new time
that can be whatever
I make it—
happy,
    sad,
good,
    bad.
Or even funny and silly!
Thank you, God—
for this beautiful
new day
and for helping me
make it whatever
I want it to be!

Father, We Thank Thee

For flowers that bloom about our feet,
Father, we thank thee,
For tender grass so fresh and sweet,
Father, we thank thee,
For the song of bird and hum of bee,
For all things fair we hear or see,
Father in heaven, we thank thee.

For blue of stream and blue of sky,
Father, we thank thee,
For pleasant shade of branches high,
Father, we thank thee,
For fragrant air and cooling breeze,
For beauty of the blooming trees,
Father in heaven, we thank thee.

For this new morning with its light,
Father, we thank thee;
For rest and shelter of the night,
Father, we thank thee;
For health and food, for love and friends,
For everything thy goodness sends,
Father in heaven, we thank thee.

—Ralph Waldo Emerson

Prayer for Peace

May this new day
bring peace and understanding
to our wonderful world.
Amen.

Starting My Day

Good morning, Lord Jesus,
I'm off to start my day.
Take my hand in your hand
And guide me in your way.

For This Day

Thank you for my sleeptime.
Thank you for this day!
I plan to laugh and smile a lot,
With lots of time to play.
And please help me remember
To also think of you.
'Cause, Jesus, I know you are here
In everything I do!

The Greatest of All Light

O God, Creator of Light,
At the rising of your sun this morning,
let the greatest of all light, your love,
rise like the sun within my heart.
Amen.

Cuddling Up

Today I woke up early, God, and our house
was so quiet. My room was cold and lonely,
so I crawled into bed with Mom and Dad. I
felt cozy and warm there, and I wasn't lonely
anymore. Thank you, God, for cozy beds and
parents to cuddle up to.

Sleepyhead

My mom called me a sleepyhead this morning, because I couldn't get out of bed.

Then a blue jay squawked outside my window. A squirrel ran by and scolded me for staying in bed so long. A dog barked across the street.

After all that, I wasn't a sleepyhead any more. Thank you for my animal alarm clock!

Counting on the New Day

One–

    I open up my eyes.

Two–

    I stretch and yawn.

Three–

    I sit up and look around.

Four–

    I thank the shining sun.

Five–

    I stand and smile so big

that *Six–*

    It lasts all day.

Seven–
  I'm going to brush my teeth.
Eight–
  I've got to go get dressed.
Nine–
  It's almost time to play!
and *Ten–*
  It's breakfast time!

And in between, I'll say,
  "Good morning, Lord!
  You've made this day so fine!"

My Friend's Birthday

I'm so excited, God. This is the day of my
friend's birthday, and I'm invited to the party.
We'll have games and cake and balloons,
and I have the coolest present to give!
Please bless my friend on this special day
and help us all to have a good time.

Good Morning, Bright Sunshine

Good morning, bright sunshine!
Come out and play again.
Our great big God is watching,
So let the fun begin!

Chapter Two

Saying Grace

When we pray, we talk to God as if we
are talking to a friend.
He loves to hear our voice any
time of the day.
Mealtimes are a very good time to
pray. We can thank God for the food
he gives us to help us grow big and
strong. At breakfast, we can also ask
him to give us a good day and help us
to make good choices all day long. At
supper, we can thank him for his help
during the day.

Give thanks whatever happens.
That is what God wants for you in Christ Jesus.
—I Thessalonians 5:18

Fill Us, Lord

Help us, Lord,
to fill our souls
as we fill our tummies,
so that we may always
be full of your love!

Come Eat with Us

God,
Come and be our guest today
And sit with us to eat.
To have you here beside us
Would make our meal complete.
Amen.

Hands and Hearts

As we join hands at our table,
    may our prayers rise to you
in praise and adoration
    and thanks for all you do.

As we join hands at our table,
    connecting heart and soul,
sharing love as we share nourishment,
    for it's love that makes us whole.

Thanks for Good Times

Dear God,

Be with us as we sit around our table,

As we eat and share the stories of our day.

Thank you for the good times and the
laughter,

The food always tastes better that way.

Wonderful Life

Thank you, Jesus,
for blessing us
with this wonderful life
and the food
you have given us.

Be with Us

The bread is pure and fresh,
the water is cool and clear.
Lord of all life, be with us,
Lord of all life, be near.

—African prayer

Let's Slow Down

Sometimes it seems as if we're always on
the go—
    going to school,
      going to lessons,
        going to practice.

Everyone has so many things to do and
so many places to go.
And so when we sit down to eat, it's a
good time to just stop and take a
    big,
        deep
           breath
and say, "Thank you, Jesus, for keeping
us safe and warm and fed."
We are so very blessed!
Amen.

Table Grace

Our table's full of food,
Our hearts are full of love,
We thank you, Heavenly Father,
For blessings from above.

Eating with Friends

Dear Jesus, thank you for the friends we
have around our table. And thank you for
the special food—especially the dessert!
We're happy to be together to eat and tell
stories. You ate with your friends, too, Lord.
Thank you for showing us how to have a
good time with each other.

Thank You, Lord

As we bow our heads to pray,
we thank you for our joy this day.

We thank you for peace
and thank you for love.
We thank you for blessings
you send from above.

No Matter

It's not important what we eat
or how pretty is our plate-full.
What matters most is that we share
and stop to say we're grateful.

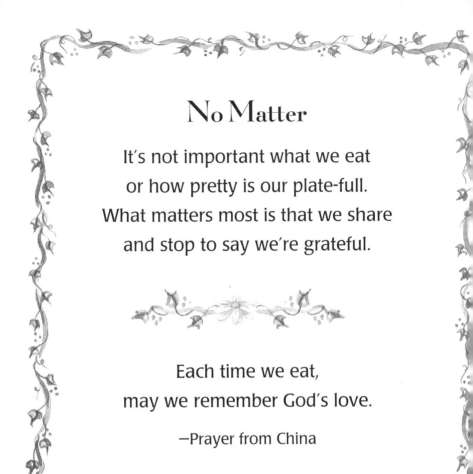

Each time we eat,
may we remember God's love.

—Prayer from China

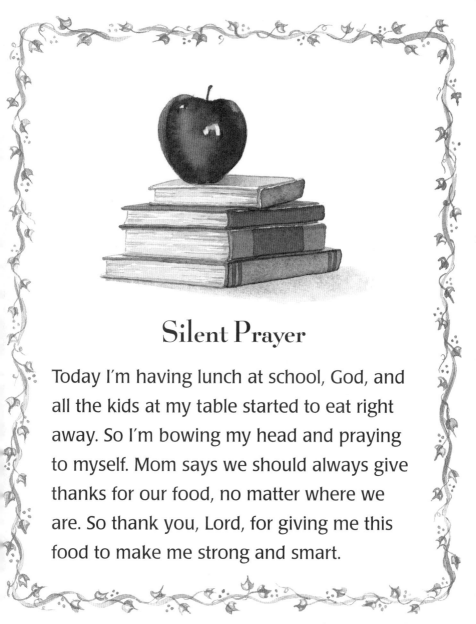

Silent Prayer

Today I'm having lunch at school, God, and all the kids at my table started to eat right away. So I'm bowing my head and praying to myself. Mom says we should always give thanks for our food, no matter where we are. So thank you, Lord, for giving me this food to make me strong and smart.

Sharing

We have lots of food at our table. We thank you for it, but we also know that there are people who don't have enough to eat. I want to share what we have with them. Please teach me how I can help those who are hungry. Amen.

Bless This Food

Father, bless the food we eat:
Bread and vegetables and fruit and meat.
Bless my family far and near,
And let them know they are so dear.

Snacks

I thank you, God, for breakfast.
I thank you, God, for lunch.
I thank you, God, for supper
And everything else I munch.

Thank You, God, for Mealtime

Thank you, God, for mealtime,
    where we share our daily bread.
Thank you for potatoes
    (though sometimes there's rice instead).

Thank you for my burger
    and chips and pickle, too.
Thank you for mac and cheese
    (though it sometimes tastes like glue).

Thank you for my veggies,
    Fresh fruit and soda pop,
For meat and fries and pizza.
    (This list will never stop!)

Thank you, God, for giving me
    these foods so good and yummy.
I know that you must love me so
    to make such food for my tummy!

Join Hands

As we share
This lovely meal
We pause to think of you—
'Cause you bring us all
That's right and good.
Thanks, God, for all you do!

Thank You for My Food

Now I thank you for my food,
rich and tasty—always good.
May it give me strength to do
all the things you want me to!

Friends Around My Table

God,

Thank you for the people around this table—

May our friendship grow each day.

Give us the strength to seek God's best for
each other,

And may we be a blessing in our words and
in our actions.

Amen.

Peanut Butter and Jelly

Thank you for my peanut butter,
and thank you for my bread.
Thank you for my jelly, too,
For by these things I'm fed.

God Is Great

God is great, God is good,
and we thank him for this food.
By his hand we all are fed,
Give us, Lord, our daily bread.

—Traditional prayer

Praise Be to God

Let us in peace eat the food
that God has provided for us.
Praise be to God for all his gifts.
Amen.

May Others Know, Too

I am so very hungry.
I cannot wait to eat!
But I know there
are some children
who I may never meet.

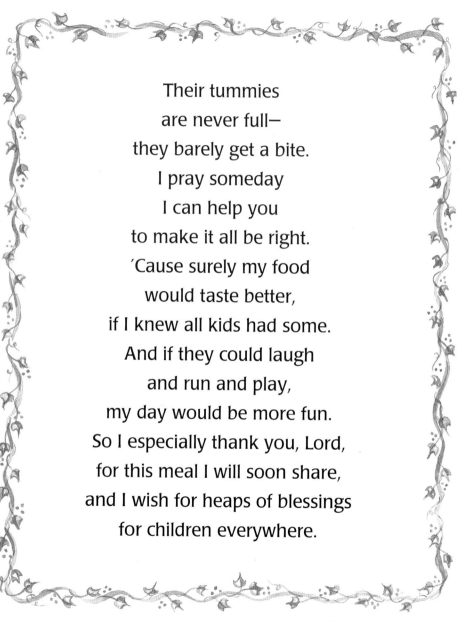

Their tummies
are never full—
they barely get a bite.
I pray someday
I can help you
to make it all be right.
'Cause surely my food
would taste better,
if I knew all kids had some.
And if they could laugh
and run and play,
my day would be more fun.
So I especially thank you, Lord,
for this meal I will soon share,
and I wish for heaps of blessings
for children everywhere.

For Those Who Make Food

Lord,
I know these yummy meals
don't just appear.
And so I send my special thanks
to those who put it here—
the farmer and the grocer
and my family, too.
And of course, thanks
    to you, Lord,
for giving me
    this food!

My Plate

I love to eat
what's on my plate.
I try not to complain.

Though sometimes
my food looks different,
when I'd rather it look the same.

I try to taste each flavor
and hope it will be great.
So thank you, God, for everything
that I find on my plate!

Food from God

As we eat our food,
Help us to remember,
It was your love, O God,
That put it here. Amen.

Our Daily Bread

Without thy sunshine and thy rain
We could not have the golden grain;
Without your love we'd not be fed;
We thank you for our daily bread.

—Anonymous

Heartfelt

When it's my turn to say grace,
All eyes rest on mine.
And even if I forget the words,
It all turns out just fine.

I don't have to be fancy
Or be afraid to start.
All I need to do is say
The feelings of my heart.

Thank You for Picnics

We bow our heads
And thank you, God, for
Each burger, dog, and bun.

We thank you, too,
For watermelon,
Salad, chips—and fun!

Friends at My Table

Thank you for my special friends
Who came to share this food.
Bless each one around me,
And make our strength renew.

For Children Everywhere

We gather here to thank you, Lord,
for food, for love, for care.
And may there always be enough
for children everywhere.

We Thank You

We thank you, Lord,
For happy hearts,
For rain and sunny weather.
We thank you, Lord,
For this our food,
And that we are together.

Come, Lord Jesus, be our guest,
And may our meal by you be blest. Amen.

—Martin Luther

Bless the Farmers

Please bless the farmers who grow
    the wheat
and the fruits and veggies that we eat.
But all who plant a garden know,
it's God who makes the garden grow.

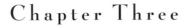

Chapter Three

Now I Lay Me Down to Sleep

We can talk to God any time. God is always ready to listen and to help us. We never have to feel alone. Bedtime is a nice, quiet time to say a prayer and spend some time with the Lord. We can thank him for the day we had or ask him for help with problems. We can praise him and celebrate the love that he gives us every day.

Morning, noon, and night I am troubled and upset. But [God] will listen to me.

–Psalm 55:17

Now I lay me down to sleep,
I pray the Lord my soul to keep.
Your love be with me through the night
And wake me with the morning light.

—Traditional prayer

Sleepy Time

Sleepy time is a special time—
the very best time
to stop and take a great, big breath
and say thank you to God for
this super-great day.

A Firefly Blessing

Dear God,
Sometimes when I look outside
my window, I see tiny blinking lights.
Mommy says they're fireflies,
but I think they're angels
coming to say, "Good night!"

Snug as a Bug

When I'm tucked in
All snug as a bug,
I've brushed my teeth
And had my hug.

When I'm tucked in,
I think of you
And ask you to bless
me
In all that I do.

Please bless my folks
And loved ones, too,
And help me be kind
In all that I do!

Alone in My Room

God, I know it's time to go to sleep, but I don't feel tired right now. Can I talk to you? Just you and me, alone in my room?

I'm sick of being too little to do things. I want to be old enough to do fun stuff like ride my bike alone to my friend's house. Mom says that I need to have patience. Will you help me to have patience, God? I need a lot! Amen.

While I'm Sleeping...

Thank you, God,
    for always being here and for watching
    over me and my family.
Thank you, God,
    for taking such good care of us today.
Thank you, God,
    for giving me the blessings of family
    and love.

The Prayer of a Happy Heart

God,

Now the day is over—
It's time to go to bed.
Keep your arms around me,
And hold my sleepy head.

Hold me tight until the dawn,
Be there when I awake.
Help me through another day,
A happy heart to make.

Amen.

Nighttime

I'm glad you made the nighttime, God. When I get tired, I need to rest. The night is quiet and dark so I can sleep. I can't see a thing in the dark. Everything seems to disappear. But in the morning everything is still where it is supposed to be. You help me get enough rest so I am ready for tomorrow. Thank you.

Bless This House

Bless this house, O Lord we pray.
Make it safe by night and day.

—Traditional prayer

A Safe World

The stars were bright when I looked at the sky tonight, Lord. They made me think of you and how you created the whole world. Please keep the world safe tonight while I'm asleep. And keep my family and me safe tonight, too. Amen.

Bedtime Is Storytime

Dear God,
Bedtime is storytime in our house. As soon as I am tucked in, my mom or dad reads the book that I pick out. I love to hear the stories. Soon I'll be able to read them all by myself. Then maybe I'll take a flashlight and read under the covers before bed. It will be like my own little world! Thank you, God, for books and for moms and dads to read them.

Blessings

It's time to ask for blessings
For my mother and my dad.
They work so hard to help me
Be good instead of bad.

They teach me all about you, God,
And tell me your stories at night
So I grow up a good child
Who knows to do what's right.

I ask you now to bless them,
And keep them close to you.
Make them strong and healthy, Lord,
And give them patience, too.
Bless Mom. Bless Dad.

Fun with Friends

Dear Father, I had fun playing games with my friends on the playground and in my yard. It was a good day. I know you were there with us, because we didn't fight at all.

Thank you, God, for my friends and my toys and all the other good things you give me to enjoy. And thanks for coming along with us and helping us to have so much fun.

Four Angels

Matthew, Mark, Luke, and John
Bless the bed that I lie on.
Four corners to my bed,
Four angels round my head,
One at the head, one at the feet,
And two to guard me while I sleep.

—Traditional prayer

Watch Over Teddy, Too

With my favorite bear beside me,
I close my eyes to rest.
Now my day is over,
I feel so richly blessed.

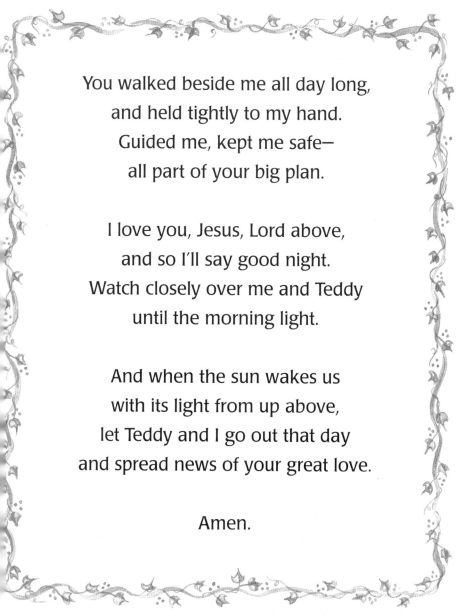

You walked beside me all day long,
and held tightly to my hand.
Guided me, kept me safe—
all part of your big plan.

I love you, Jesus, Lord above,
and so I'll say good night.
Watch closely over me and Teddy
until the morning light.

And when the sun wakes us
with its light from up above,
let Teddy and I go out that day
and spread news of your great love.

Amen.

Sleeping Over

I thought it would be fun to sleep at my friend's house, but now I'm not so sure. I'm lonesome for my mom and dad. My tummy even sort of hurts. Please make the ache go away. Help me feel better so I can sleep and my dad won't have to come and get me until morning.

A Busy Day

Dear God,

I had a busy day today. Mom says I need to get right to bed so I won't be grumpy and grouchy in the morning. Nobody likes a grouch, especially me. Please help me get plenty of sleep so I'll wake up happy. Good night!

Now the Day Is Over

Now the day is over;
Night is drawing nigh.
Shadows of the evening
Steal across the sky.

Jesus, give the weary
Calm and sweet repose;
With your tenderest blessing
May my eyelids close.

Through the long night watches,
May your angels spread
Their white wings above me,
Watching around my bed.

When the morning wakens,
Then may I arise
pure and fresh and sinless
In your holy eyes.

–Sabine Baring-Gould

Time to Snuggle

When it's time
to snuggle up
and turn the lights real low,

I think of you
up in the heavens
and all the stuff you know.

You really see it all, Lord,
when you look down
from above,

And everything you see
you fill
with your great love!

A Good Day

I woke up in the morning, I was happy
all day long,
I never said an ugly word but smiled
and played along.
And now at last I see the sun setting in
the west,
And I am very happy, for I know I've
done my best.

Lights Out!

Lord, it's time to turn the light out and go to sleep. Thank you for being by my side all day and keeping me safe. I would give you a hug, but you're too big. I can only wrap the blanket around me and pretend that your arms are holding me. I love you, God!

Thank You for the Moon

Thank you for the moon above
That shines into my room.
Thank you for the stars that glow,
They shatter any gloom.
Thank you for the quietness,
I feel my heart at peace.
Resting here within your care,
My troubles are released.

The Dark

Everything is dark and spooky in my room tonight, Lord. I hear thumpy, bumpy sounds. Creepy shadows move across my wall. Please stay with me until morning and keep me safe. Help me so I won't be afraid.

Day Is Done

Day is done.
Gone the sun
From the lakes,
From the hills,
From the sky.

All is well.
Safely rest,
God is nigh.

—Unknown

A Better Day...

Today, was not my best day, Lord.
I wasn't always good.

But tomorrow I'll be better
and do everything I should!

I See the Moon

I see the moon,
⠀⠀⠀⠀And the moon sees me;
God bless the moon,
⠀⠀⠀⠀And God bless me.

—Anonymous

Summer Concerts

Dear God,
Through my open window,
I hear the crickets singing.
Their music is so beautiful.
It's like violins singing me to sleep.
The crickets must be sending signals
    to each other.
Or maybe they're praying:
"Sleep tight! And God bless
    everyone tonight."

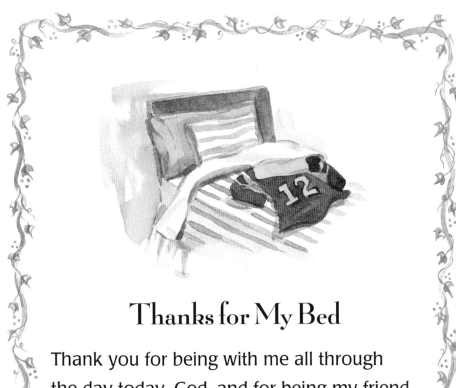

Thanks for My Bed

Thank you for being with me all through
the day today, God, and for being my friend.
Thank you for my bed and a good night's
sleep. Some kids in the world don't have a
bed with warm, fuzzy blankets like mine. Be
their friend, too, Lord, and please keep them
comfortable. Amen.

Bless the Children

Dear Lord, please help me to learn about you every day and to lead the kind of life that will make you and my family so very proud of me. I want people to see the good of you shining out from me. Amen.

My Day

As I climb into bed
and lay down my head,
it's time to remember
my day.

All the things that I've done,
the work and the fun.
And now is the best time
to pray—

I pray for your love
that comes from above.
Please help me and show me
your way.

Tomorrow Is Another Day

I lay my sleepy head down,
My busy day is done.
Tomorrow is another day
I hope to fill with fun.

If you are there beside me
Leading me on my way,
I know that it will surely be
A grand and glorious day!

May the Night Bring Peace

Dearest Jesus,

Please keep everyone safe
and comfy and warm,
and may we wake up
to a world filled with peace.

Amen.

Good Night, Stars

God, the night is so quiet and peaceful. I can hear myself breathing. I love to squeeze my teddy bear and look up at the stars. Good night, stars. Good night, moon. Good night, God.

Guide Me, Angels

Guard me, guide me, angels,
hide me from the troubles all around.
Keep me safe and give me faith
to hear your steps in every sound.

I Love You, God

I love you in the morning
before I go to play.
I love you when it's noontime,
and lunch is on the way.
I love you when it's dark outside,
and I am dressed for bed.
I love you all day long, God—
You're always in my head!

Children of the World

As I get ready to go to sleep,
I like to stop for a minute
and think of all the wonderful ways
that you have blessed me.

And I think of those, too, Lord,
who aren't as lucky as I,
and I pray that you will keep
them in your sight,
so that all the children of the world
may one day go to bed
with a heart full of hope.

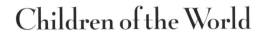

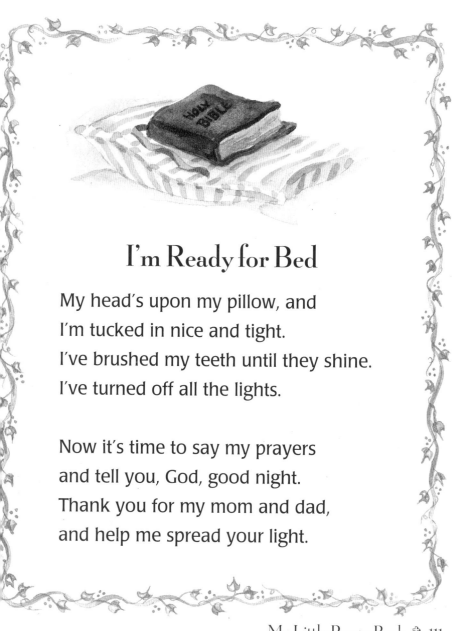

I'm Ready for Bed

My head's upon my pillow, and
I'm tucked in nice and tight.
I've brushed my teeth until they shine.
I've turned off all the lights.

Now it's time to say my prayers
and tell you, God, good night.
Thank you for my mom and dad,
and help me spread your light.

Thanks, God!

Hey, God—
Today was a great day,
and I just wanna say:
Thanks.
'Night!

Bless Those I Love

Please bless my mom and my dad,
and all the people I love.
Send sweet blessings down to them
from your home way up above.

Good Night

Good night! Good night!
Far flies the light;
But still God's love
Shall flame above,
Making all bright.
Good night! Good night!

—Victor Hugo

Chapter Four

Guide Me, Father

Some days are tough, and we need God's help. Maybe we feel sick or we aren't getting along with someone, or maybe we are just having a bad day. God knows the solution to any problem. He can do things that no one else can.
All we have to do is ask him for help.

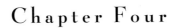

*I call to you in times of trouble. You
certainly will answer me.*

—Psalm 86:7

When I'm Afraid, I Call Your Name

Sometimes when things are not quite right
And I get so very afraid,
I quickly call your name, dear Lord,
And the fear just seems to fade.

But I am always with you. You have held my hand. You guide me with your advice. And later you will receive me in honor.

—Psalm 73:23–24

Watch Over Me

Today wasn't the easiest day, Lord,
but I try to remember
that you are with me
no matter what
and that sometimes
the hard days
teach me the most.

Please watch over me
while I am sleeping
and help me
find a way
to make
tomorrow better.

Listening with My Heart

Dear God,
I know you're busy
And you've got so much to do,
But there's something I don't understand
And I need some help from you....

So I am going to pray really hard
And listen with my heart—
Because when I have a problem,
That's where I always start!

Help Me to Be My Best

Help me, God, to be my best
In everything I do.
I want you to be proud of me
And be a blessing, too.
Amen.

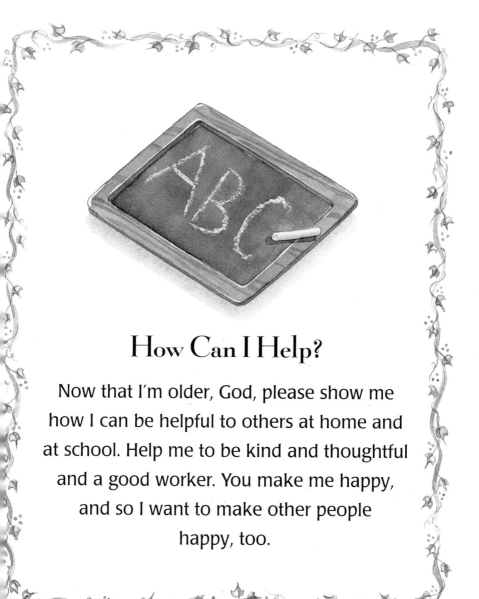

How Can I Help?

Now that I'm older, God, please show me
how I can be helpful to others at home and
at school. Help me to be kind and thoughtful
and a good worker. You make me happy,
and so I want to make other people
happy, too.

Trying Something New

Dear Lord,

When I was little I was afraid to try new things, like riding my bike without training wheels or putting my face underwater in the pool. But now I know you are with me and you tell me not to be afraid. When I pray, you make me braver. Stay near me, Lord, and I can do all kinds of new things with your help.

I'm Sad Today...

I'm feeling so very sad today.
I wish you could take
My sadness away.

Please just listen and understand,
Send me your love and hold my hand.
Help me to be strong and help me to know—
This sad part of life will help me to grow.

Disappointment

Dear God, I feel sad and alone today. My friend was supposed to come play with me, but he couldn't come. I am so disappointed and mad. I don't like feeling like that.

Please take away my bad feelings, Lord. Help me not to be so upset. I know you are my friend and that you are always here with me. Could you please help me to be happier?

Lead Me Day by Day

I thank you for your help
that leads me on my way.
I want to follow you, dear Lord,
all throughout my days.

Give Me What I Ask

Please give me what I ask, dear Lord,
if you'd be glad about it.
But if you think it's not for me,
please help me do without it.

—Traditional prayer

Saying Hurtful Things

God, sometimes I say hurtful things when I don't really mean to say them. Help me to be careful of what I say and to forgive others when they are not kind to me. Amen.

Being Truthful

Sometimes it's hard to tell the truth, God. Especially when my mom asks if I took a cookie or something like that. I don't want her to be mad. But you expect me to be honest, Lord, and admit when I have done something wrong. I'm not very good at it now. If you help me, I'll do better.

Show Me Your Way

Jesus,
Please show me your light
And show me the way.
Help me to find you
Each time I pray.

Dealing with Meanies

Dear Jesus, someone in my class hurt me. I wanted to hurt the person back, but I didn't because I knew you wouldn't like it. You want us to love one another. Sometimes that is *hard.* I need help from you, Lord, to love someone who is mean to me.

I Miss My Pet

Dear Lord,
My special pet has died
And I'm so very sad.
I've lost the best buddy
A kid has ever had.

I pray that you will guard
    her soul
'Cause I know that this is true—
That though I feel so very sad
Her spirit's safe
    with you.

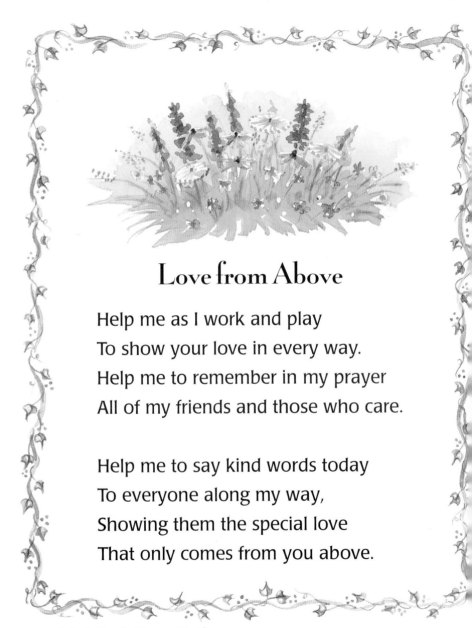

Love from Above

Help me as I work and play
To show your love in every way.
Help me to remember in my prayer
All of my friends and those who care.

Help me to say kind words today
To everyone along my way,
Showing them the special love
That only comes from you above.

A Grouchy Day

I feel grouchy today, God. I don't want to be nice. Help me remember that you sometimes had bad days, too. What did you do about it? I want to be like you, so help me feel better and not so grumpy. Thanks. Amen.

Losing My Temper

Dear Jesus, why do I get angry so easily?
You are strong, Lord. Help me to be strong,
too, so I don't lose my temper. You want me
to treat others the way I want to be treated.
Take my hand, Lord. Show me how. Help me
to be more like you.

Be Thou My Guardian and My Guide

Be thou my guardian and my guide,
And hear me when I call;
Let not my slippery footsteps slide,
And hold me lest I fall.

—Isaac Williams

The Good Shepherd

The Lord is like a shepherd,
He watches over the land.
He keeps his flock from danger,
Protected by his hand.

I want to follow you, Lord,
Each and every day.
Help me listen to your words
And never let me stray.

I'm So Confused

Life can be confusing, Lord,
I don't know what to do.
Please help me understand it,
'Cause I believe in you!

God's Forgiveness

Lord, you are always ready to forgive me. When I do wrong things, you give me another chance. You put a new spirit inside me, so I can try again to do things right. Help me to forgive others the way you do. Amen.

A Good Player

Good Lord,
help me to win if I may,
and if I may not,
help me to be a good loser.

Sharing

Father, I'm sorry that I was so selfish and wouldn't let my friend ride my bike. Now I'm not allowed to ride my bike at all until I learn how to share better. I'm sorry for all the times I didn't share. I want to do what is right. Help me, God, to follow you and do what you would do.

Everyone Seems So Sad

I wish that I could cheer them up
And somehow make things right.
All the grown-ups seem so sad,
There's something wrong tonight.

Please bless them all
And send your love.
Lord, I pray this much to you—
That your great love will shine down
And faith will see them through.

The Little Children

Jesus loves the little children,
All the children of the world.
Red and yellow, black and white,
They are precious in his sight.
Jesus loves the little children of the world.

—C. Herbert Woolston

Help Me Today

Jesus, I try not to ask too much.
Instead, I like to pray for others,
but today I really need your help.
I pray you will show me the way.

My Friend Needs You

Lord,
My friend needs your support today
So I'm coming to you in prayer
That you might find a way to show
My friend how much you care.

Sometimes It's Hard to Pray

Sometimes it seems so hard to pray, Jesus. I feel silly or stupid or, I don't know…strange. It just doesn't always seem right. So I'm going to keep trying. While I am doing that, will you keep listening? Thank you.

Things Are Going Well

Things are going really well,
So all I want to say
Is that I would surely like your help
In keeping it that way!

I Have Faith

Lately, Lord,
people aren't always
being so nice
to each other
in this big, wide world.
But I have faith
that one day soon
things will be better—
I have faith in people,
I have faith in myself,
and most of all,
I have faith in you
and your gentle goodness.

When Words Hurt

Dear God, I don't always say the right thing. Sometimes I say bad things to other people. Help me to stop before I say words that hurt someone's feelings. I want to say kind words. Maybe if I do, people will be nicer to me, too. Amen.

For My Dad

Dear God, my dad is sick today. Help me to do things that will make him feel better so he can get well and do all of his dad-things again. Thanks, God. Amen.

Sharing with God

Dear God,
Please bless the gift I gave
at Sunday School
today.
May it help
many people
all around the world.
Help me to be generous, Lord,
and to remember that
everything I own
really belongs to you.

Good Manners

My mom says good manners make the day go better. They also show that you respect other people. Sometimes I forget to be polite, but I know it is important. If I want someone to be polite to me, I have to show them how. Please guide me to be the kind of person I should be—pleasant and polite.

Unselfishness

Dear God,

Come into my heart and teach me to be unselfish. Help me think of others and not just myself. Fill me with your love and make me willing to share. This is sometimes really hard for me.

Show Me the Way

Dear Jesus,
show me how to live—
to share your love
and learn to give.

Dear Jesus,
show me how to be
the nicest, kindest,
most wonderful me!

With You Beside Me

An older kid at school is mean to me. He says not to tell. I'm scared. Lord, please keep me safe and help me know how to act and what to do. I know that if you are beside me, I can get through this and maybe even ask someone for help.

Praying for Peace

I really don't like fighting and shouting.
Please let me help you make a peaceful
world. Show me how to be friendly and
unselfish and to help people get along. Put
your peace inside me, so I can pass it on.
I know that others will see your goodness
shining out from me.

Chapter Five

Talks with God

We get to know people by talking
to them. We can do the same thing
with God. We learn about God by
talking to him and by reading the
Bible. We learn that he loves us and
is interested in everything we do.
He helps us be kind to others and forgives
us when we do bad things.

The Lord our God comes near
when we pray to him.

—Deuteronomy 4:7

Talking Things Out

Sometimes the world seems wacky
When things aren't going right.
And it helps to know you're here
To keep us in your sight.

I know you're always listening
And you'll always show the way.
Whenever I talk things out with you,
It becomes a better day!

I Wonder...

Dear Lord,
Sometimes I wonder if you're there
'Cause I look up and just see air.
I know you're busy, so much to do,
And I try so hard to believe in you.
I try to have faith that you ARE there—
Even when I look up and just see air.

*Then the people brought their little children
to Jesus so that he could put his hands on
them and pray for them. When his followers saw
this, they told the people to stop bringing their
children to Jesus. But Jesus said, 'Let the little
children come to me. Don't stop them,
because the kingdom of heaven belongs to
people who are like these children.'*

—Matthew 19:13–14

Everything I Do

Lord, you are in everything I do.
My words and thoughts are touched by you.
When I'm in a time of need,
My prayers I send to you with speed.
Help me build a life that's strong
To make me feel like I belong.
Lord, I love you—you're in my heart.
And I know that we will never part.

I've Got a Question

Dear Lord,
I've got a question
that I'm dying to ask you—
you see, I've always wondered
just what is it you do?

I know you're up in heaven,
and you watch over us below.
But I still don't get it, God,
and I really want to know.

I mean, do you play cards at night
or ever watch TV?
And do you paint each rainbow
especially for me?

You see, I know you're busy Sundays
when we go to church and pray,
But, God, could you just tell me—
do you ever get to play?

This Little Light of Mine

This little light of mine,
I'm gonna let it shine.
Oh, this little light of mine,
I'm gonna let it shine.
This little light of mine,
I'm gonna let it shine.
Let it shine!
Let it shine!
Let it shine!

—African American spiritual

Fill My Heart with Joy

Fill my heart with joy, God,
in each and every way.
So I can show the world your love
with each new passing day.

Talking to God

God, is talking to you like talking on the telephone? I like to talk to friends and family on the phone. It seems that they are right in the room with me. I like to feel that close to you, God. I can tell you all about my day. Amen.

Help Me, God

I don't know why you love me
'Cause sometimes I am so bad,
But you are there to help me,
That makes my heart so glad!

When I'm tempted to do things
I know I should not do.
Be there to help me out, God,
So I can be like you.

Sad Days, Glad Days

Some days are sad,
Some days are glad,
Some days I feel so very mad.

But you are there
To love and care
And all my problems you will bear.

A Sick Day

Dear Lord,
I'm not feeling good today, and I have
to stay in bed. My mom says she's your
assistant. I know she'll take good care of me.
Please stay near me, Lord, and help me feel
better.

Be Kind to One Another

Help me, God, to be kind to others. If they don't have any money and can't buy the things they need, help me to share and be a friend. Amen.

A Little Bit of Kindness

A little bit of kindness
Goes a long, long way
To cheer a very sad heart
And help a friend today.

So help me, God, to always see
A person who is sad.
I'll cheer him up!
I'll make him smile!
I'll make his heart so glad.

Special Children

Dear God,

We have some special children in our
school who can't learn easily. The other kids
make fun of them. I don't think that's fair.
They are all your children, Lord. You made
them, and you love them.

Please protect your special
children. Help me be
kind and friendly
to them. Then
maybe other
kids will do
the same.

Are You Listening?

Dear Lord,
I've been praying really hard,
    been talking to you each day.
But sometimes I still wonder
    if you hear the things I say.
And just when I am doubting,
    just when I want to know,
I'll look into the blue sky
    and see a perfect rainbow.
And then I know you've
    heard me and then I'm
    sure you care.
Because then I am reminded
    that you are
    everywhere!

Make Grandpa Well

Lord, my grandpa is sick. I'm scared, God. What if something happens to him? Please watch over my grandpa and make him well so we can have all of our fun together again. Amen.

Do the Right Thing

Dear God, I'm so confused. I don't know the right thing to do. I want to do one thing when I know I should do another. Next time I have a problem, help me stop and think and pray. Remind me to ask myself what you'd do, Lord.

How Big Are You, God?

How big are you, God?
Are you taller than a tree?
Do you jump over mountains
or play in the blue sea?
I would really like to know,
if you could answer, please.
How does a great and awesome God
love a little kid like me?

I Feel You, God

I can hear you in the night
When crickets make their sounds.
I can feel you in the wind
That blows the leaves around.
I can see you in the rain
That falls upon the ground.

I know you're everywhere, God,
In everything I see.
What a super miracle—
That you can dwell in me!

Other Children, Other Places

Dear God,
We hear so much about
other parts of the world,
places where children
do not have families
and homes
and food.
And so today, I don't want to ask
for anything for me.
I want to ask you
to watch over
all those children
and make sure
they are okay.

Jesus Loves Me

Jesus loves me! This I know,
   For the Bible tells me so.
Little ones to Him belong;
   They are weak but He is strong.
Yes, Jesus loves me.
Yes, Jesus loves me.
Yes, Jesus loves me.
The Bible tells me so.

—Anna B. Warner

Just Me

Dear God,

I know it is wrong to want what someone else has, but sometimes I just can't help it. Like a kid on my street has a better bike than mine, and I really want it. Come into my heart, Lord, and take away these bad feelings. Make me happy to be just me.

A Prayer for My Mom

Dear God,
Please look out for my mom,
She needs your loving hand.
She is such a special mother,
Who always understands.

But, God, you know she works hard,
She never seems to rest.
So please look out for my mom,
Because she is the best!

Can You...

Can you help a little child
Who fell off her bike today?
Can you heal her knees and elbows
And take the pain away?

Can you listen as I tell
My secrets to you, Lord?
Please keep them deep within
your heart
And let my spirit
soar!

Nothin' Much

Not too much going on today.
Don't really have a thing to say.
But when I looked into the sky,
It made me want to just say "Hi!"

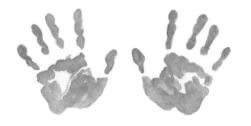

Forgive Me, Jesus

I pray for your forgiveness
For what I did today.
I promise to be better,
And I really want to say
That I didn't mean to do it.
It just happened. Well, okay,
I know that it was my fault—
But I'm fixing it today!

What Do You Look Like, God?

Do you have a body?
Do you look like me?
Can you throw a football?
Can you climb a tree?

Can you swing upon a star
and make the moon shine bright?
Can you listen to my prayers
when I turn out the light?

All these things I want to know
so answer please, I pray.
I want to get a picture
of how you are today.

A New Person

Dear Father,

I try to do the things I should, but sometimes I don't do them. Teach me how to live the way you want me to. Please forgive me for all the wrong things I do and make me a new person.

What a Friend

What a friend we have in Jesus,
All our sins and griefs to bear!
What a privilege to carry
Everything to God in prayer!

Oh, what peace we often forfeit,
Oh, what needless pain we bear,
All because we do not carry
Everything to God in prayer.

—Joseph Scriven

Help to Make It Better

Dear God,

Please bless my special friend
today who's feeling really ill.
Please help to make it better,
I pray that it's your will.

Amen.

Help Me Be Strong

Dear God,
Teach me to be strong. When sad things happen to me, help me keep my mind on you. Show me what I can do to turn a bad thing into something good.

I Love You, God

Just want you to know,
That I love you so!

What Can I Give Him?

What can I give him,
Poor as I am?
If I were a shepherd,
I would bring a lamb;
If I were a wise man,
I would do my part;
Yet what can I give him—
Give him my heart.

—Christina Rossetti

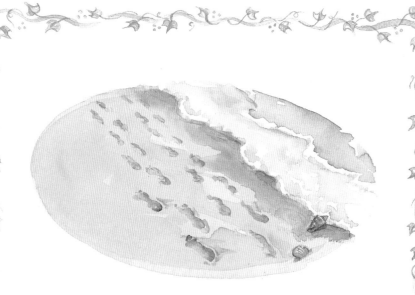

You Are with Me

Dear God,

You tell me not to be afraid because you are with me. I forget that sometimes. Then I feel scared. It's not fun to be frightened. Please help me remember I am not alone. You are right beside me all the time.

Thanks for Listening

Dear God, I like having you with me all day long. I like the way you let me talk to you, especially when things go wrong. I feel better just telling you what's on my mind. Thanks for sharing yourself with me.

So Good to Know

Lord,
It's just so very good to know
That you are here to help me grow.

I Belong to God

Dear Jesus,

You give me all the things I need. I love you and put my trust in you. Teach me to be helpful, kind, and gentle. Help me care about others and obey my parents. Then everyone will know I belong to you.

I'm Sorry

You wouldn't be proud of me today, God. I called my friend a bad name. I didn't mean to make my friend sad. I didn't mean to say such ugly things.

I said "I'm sorry," but I want to tell you that I am sorry, too. I need your help for next time, so I won't act mean and hurt someone's feelings again.

Take Time to Be Holy

Take time to be holy.
Speak often with your Lord;
Abide in Him always,
And feed on His Word.
Make friends of God's children;
Help those who are weak,
Forgetting in nothing His blessing to seek.

—W. D. Longstaff

When I Pray to You

When I pray to you, Jesus Christ,
my fingers fold together as if
to say "Hello" to one another,
just as I am saying "Hello" to you.

Where Do You Live, God?

Do you live among the mountains?
Do you live along the sea?
Do you live among the cornstalks
That tip their hats to me?
Do you live among the tall, green pines
Or in a meadow fair?
I do know where you live, God,
You're here and everywhere!

Chapter Six

Thanks Be to God

When we say "thank you" to God, we are giving him praise. We are saying, "You're the greatest" and "You're cool, God." Everyone likes to get praise, and so does our God. He has done so many good things for us; we should praise him every day.

Let everything that breathes praise the Lord.
Praise the Lord!

—Psalm 150:6

I'm Thankful for You!

I'm thankful for the moon and stars.
I'm thankful for the sea.
I'm thankful for the hugs I get.
I'm thankful to be me!
I'm thankful for the morning.
I'm thankful for the night.
I'm thankful for the days
When everything goes right.

I'm thankful for my family
And its never-ending love.
And most of all I'm thankful
For *you,* watching over from above.

I Notice You, God

God,
Sometimes I feel
no one notices me,
and I wonder if you
feel that way, too.

So I just want to say
thank you—
I sure notice all that you do!

Your Great Love

Thank you, God, for the sun above
That warms my heart with your great love,
Reminding me you're always there
To answer even my smallest prayer.

Father, Son, and Holy Ghost

Praise God, from whom all blessings flow;
Praise Him, all creatures here below;
Praise Him above, you heavenly host;
Praise Father, Son, and Holy Ghost.

–Thomas Ken

Thank You for the Bible

God, thank you for the Bible. I like all the stories. It helps me to know who you are and how you care for me. It tells me all about your followers—Moses, David, Mary, and Paul. Help me to grow up to be like those good people. That would be cool. Amen.

You're Awesome

You're incredible, God!
There is no one quite like you.
Who else could do the
Great things that you do?

Now, our God, we thank you.
And we praise your glorious name.

−1 Chronicles 29:13

I Like Learning About You

God, thank you for my church where I can learn about you. Thank you for my pastor and teachers who help me to understand the Bible. It is a very big book, God, but I'll try to read it every day. Amen.

A Special Treasure

I am your special treasure,
unique in every way.
I'm thankful that you made me
on that important day.

Help me to grow big and strong
and follow after you.
I'll do the things that please you most
and spread your message, too.

Amen.

Thank You for My Dog

Thank you for my dog, God,
He is such a good friend.
We share all kinds of secrets,
Our love just never ends.

We sometimes run and tumble
In the green grass of our lawn.
He licks my face with kisses
'Til my sadness is all gone.

My Body, Strong and Good

I have two eyes that wink and blink,
I have a mind to help me think,
I have two hands that clap for fun,
I have two feet that jump and run,
I have two ears to hear a song,
Two lips to praise him all day long,
I have a body strong and good,
To use for Jesus as I should.

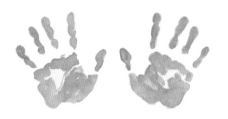

I'm Counting on You!

It's hard to count all my blessings, God. Sometimes it seems easier to just tell you about a problem I'm having because then I wouldn't have to count so high! I am thankful for what you give me. I do notice my blessings. Thank you for the goodness in my life.

My Parents Are the Best

I've got the best parents
a kid's ever had—
thanks for my mother
and thanks for my dad!

I Want to Sing

Dear God,

You make me so happy
that I want to sing.
I want to sing
about your love
and all the good things
you do for me.
You take care of me
and give me all that I need.
You help and guide me.

Lord, I will sing about
your love forever.

So Good to Me

I haven't said this for awhile—
I don't know how long it's been.
So I hope you won't mind much
if I say it all again.

You have been so good to me
and to my family, too,
we just want to say thank you
for all the things you do!

Taking the Time

I've been really busy
    with school and sports
    and family things,
so I haven't
taken much time to pray
to you lately, God.

I don't mean to take
    my blessings
    for granted.
I really do
notice everything
you do for me.

Thank you, Lord.

God's Care

I praise you, Father, for giving us all of the things our family needs. You give us our food, drink, clothing, a place to live, and people to love us. God, you take good care of us. Amen.

The Very Best

Wow—
I'm sure blessed!
God, you're the best!

Each Day Is a Blessing

Each morning when I open up my eyes,
I see you've created a new sunrise.
Each day is a blessing, each day a surprise
when I wake up and open my eyes!

A Loving God

God, you are awesome,
   you really are the best—
even when I'm bad
   and put you to the test.

God, you are great
   in all the things you do.
Thank you, loving God,
   for being wonderful you!

Creation

Dear Lord,

You made the world out of *nothing.*

You made the day and night,

the sky, the earth, and the water.

You made the stars, moon, and sun

and covered the world

with plants and animals.

Then you made people.

How did you do all that, Lord?

It was a BIG job.

You are a mighty God!

God Is Strong

Dear God,
You are so strong,
You are like a rock.
When I need to be strong,
I know I can pray to you.
Then you will answer
And make me strong, too.

Thank You for My Church

Thank you for my pastor,
He's kind and nice and good.
He helps me know your word
And live the way I should.

Thank you for my teacher
Who explains about your ways.
We sing and pray and color,
And hear tales of Bible days.

God's Healing

My mom was sick, but now she's okay.
Thank you, God, for answering my prayers
and making her well. You take care of us
every day, Lord. We ask for your help, and
you give it. You make us all feel better. I am
so glad we have you with us.

Praise the Lord Today

When we go to church on Sunday,
I love to sing your praise—
But what about the blessings
We receive on other days?

So though it isn't Sunday,
I thought it right to say—
Thank you for the blessings
You have given us today!

Thanks for My Home

I praise you, Lord, for my home. It is cozy and warm in the winter and cool in the summer. It's a great home, and I know all the secret places to hide. Everything here makes me feel good. Thank you, Lord. You always know just what I need.

It's All Because of You

What makes the earth spin?
What makes the grass grow?
What makes the stars shine?
What makes the birds fly?
What makes our hearts full?
What gives our souls peace?
What fills us with song?
What makes us ask *Why?*

What makes us so sure
that after winter will come spring?
It's you, Jesus, you!
'Cause you do everything!

God Takes Care of Us

You know everything about me, Lord. You send me food and clothes when I need them. You cheer me up when I'm sad and heal me when I'm sick. How do you do all of that?

You do everything for me because you love me. Thank you for watching over me, Lord. Thank you for caring.

God's Love

Thank you for your love, Lord.
You made me.
I belong to you.
If I forget about you,
you never forget me.
Even when I'm naughty,
you still love me.
Your love lasts forever
and ever.
You are a great God.

God of Comfort

Dear God,

I know you will be with me if I am in trouble.
You promise to take away my sadness. It
makes me feel better to know that I can
count on you to help me through sad times!
Thank you, Lord, for your promise.

Sunday School

Thank you for my Sunday school,
    where friends can meet and play
And listen to the word of God
    to help us find our way.

Thank you for the projects
    we color, cut, and glue.
We make something beautiful
    that reminds us all of you.

We Give Our Thanks

We give our thanks to you today,
For you have blessed us in every way.
Help us to do the things we should,
And remember to be kind and good.

God's Protection

I give thanks to you, O Lord, for taking care
of me. You protect me and keep me safe. I
trust you because I know you love me and
will never leave me.

Thank You for My Teddy Bear

God,
Thank you for my teddy bear,
I squeeze him every night.
I like to take him with me
And hold him really tight.
Amen.

Thank You, God, for Everything

Thank you, God, for everything
I have within my room—
    the books and toys and magazines
    all bring me so much fun.

Thank you, God, for everything
I have within my house—
    the fridge, the TV, the microwave,
    they help us out a ton.

Thank you, God, for everything
I have within my world—
    the park, the pool, the playground
    where I can play and run.

Chapter Seven

My Family

God has given each of us a family to love and respect. It's hard to get along with brothers and sisters, but he has given us this practice time to learn how to live in harmony with all people. God also wants us to pray for our family. He knows he can count on us to do the job.

The Lord is close to everyone who prays to him,
to all who truly pray to him.

—Psalm 145:18

Bless Our Family

Please come into our home and bless our family, God. Protect us and teach us how to take good care of each other. Fill our home with your love so everyone who visits will see how happy our life with you is! Amen.

A Family Prayer

Here we are, God,
look at us!
We've all joined hands to pray.
Everyone has something
that they really want to say.
So please listen to our prayers
as we gather to let you know—
that you, God, are our guiding light,
and we all love you so!

My Heritage

I like to think of my family
    going back so very far.
Those great-great-great-great-grandparents
    don't know how great they are!
If it wasn't for those people,
    where would my family be?
It took those folks so long ago
    to start our family tree!

My Parents

Some parents do a little.
Some parents do a lot.
Some buy their kids a bunch of stuff—
And some of them do not.

But when it comes to parents, God,
Mine stand out from the rest.
I've just got to thank you, Lord,
For giving me the best!

My Family's Different

There are so many different
kinds of families,
and I know you love each one.
Mine is not the standard format,
but we sure do have some fun.

Yet, Lord, it isn't always easy
and sometimes you know I pray
that we'd be more like others,
but I know that's not your way.

For everyone is different
so I'll try not to make a fuss—
because I know that you've created
a family that is just right for us!

Thank You for Grandma and Grandpa

Thank you for my grandma, God,
And for my grandpa, too.
I love them oh so dearly.
And they love me as you do.

They help me know I'm special,
And encourage me each day
To always follow you, God,
And never go astray.

The Ones I Love

Dear God, I'm glad you gave me a family to love and care for me. You knew I would be lonely if I didn't have them. Help me to be kind and gentle to all those who love me. Then they will know I love them back.

Peace

God, please bring peace to my house and to all of us who live there. Please keep us from fighting too much and remind us how much we love and care for each other. Amen.

Mom's Love

Dear God,
My mom has the
softest touch
    and warmest hugs
    of anyone in the world.
She takes such good care of me!
When I'm sad, she snuggles me in her arms
    and whispers in my ear
    and kisses me.
Soon I'm smiling again.
She loves me
    just like you do, Lord.
    Did she learn how from you?
Thank you, God, for my mom.

Honoring My Parents

Jesus,
You know I love my mommy,
you know I love my dad.
They're about the coolest parents
a kid has ever had.

But still sometimes I yell
and still I do get mad
and talk back to my mommy
or say things to my dad.
So, Jesus, please watch over me
so I'll be a better kid.
Then I won't have to ask forgiveness
for something that I did.

'Cause you know I love my mom,
and I love my dad, too.
And most of all, dear Jesus,
you know that I love you!

Family

Nothing's more important
Right from the very start,
Than the family who loves you
And keeps you in their heart!

My Daddy

Be with my daddy, God,
Wherever he may be.
Keep him safe within your arms
'Til he comes back to me.

My Sister

My sister plays school with me and teaches me new words. We even do craft projects together. She shows me how. Sometimes she acts like she's my mom, but that's okay. Thank you, Father, for giving me a sister who loves me and takes care of me.

My Brother

Sometimes my brother is a pain, Jesus. You had brothers, so you know what I mean. But he makes me laugh, too. And he plays with me and helps me with my spelling. So I'm glad to have him around. Thank you for my brother.

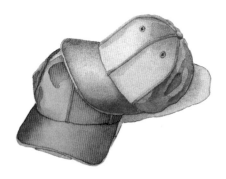

I Sought My Brother

I sought my soul,
but my soul I could not see.
I sought my God,
but my God eluded me.
I sought my brother,
and found all three.

—Unknown

A Special Treasure

Thanks, God, for my mom. She always seems to know how to make things better. When a kid at school laughed at the way I look, Mom said that you made every person a special treasure and that each treasure can look different. That's cool, God.

Grandparents Are Special

Dear Lord, Thank you for my grandparents. They always have time to read to me or play games. They like to tickle and play and laugh. And they like ice cream and going to the park, too.

Mostly though, God, they love me. Please take care of them, Lord, I think they must be a lot like you.

Thank You for My Family

Thank you for my parents
and for my brothers, too.
They teach me to ride my bike
and how to tie my shoes.

They make me sausage pizza.
Sometimes we play a game.
I couldn't live without them.
It would not be the same.

We Can All Get Along

Sometimes we argue.
Sometimes we fight.
But with your help,
We'll make it be right.

We fight too much.
I know that it's wrong.
But with your help,
We can all get along.

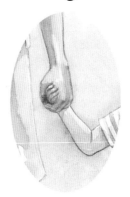

Thank You for My Mom

Thank you for my mom, dear Lord.
She loves me every minute,
Even when I'm not so good
And test her to the limit.

Great-Grandma

Dear God,

My great-grandma keeps getting shorter. I'm almost as tall as she is now! She has to hold my arm when she walks. Help me to take good care of her, Lord. She's very old, but she's the best back-scratcher in the world, and she always tells me great stories.

Baby Sister

God, thank you for my sister.
I'm glad she's here with me.
She is so sweet and cuddly,
As cute as she could be!

I prayed to you for a sister,
Asked you to send a girl
To be my friend forever—
A precious little pearl.

And now she's here beside me,
So dear and oh so sweet.
As a present from you, dear God,
My sister just can't be beat!

Sleeping Over

Tomorrow is the day I'm sleeping over at
Grandma's, God. I can't wait. Grandma
fixes all my favorite foods. Then she plays
with me. We paint pictures together, and
if it isn't raining, we go for a walk and talk
about how you made the whole world.

I love my grandma, Lord, and she loves
me. She says we love each other because
you first loved us.

My Parents Work Hard

Dear Jesus,
My parents work very hard
to give me the things
I need and want.
Please help me to be good
so that their lives are
a little easier.
Thank you, Lord.
Amen.

Thank You for Aunts and Uncles

Thank you for my many aunts
And for my uncles, too.
They give me hugs and kisses
And tell me "I love you!"

Those I Love

God bless all those that I love.
God bless all those that love me.
God bless all those that love those that I love,
And all those that love those that love me.

—New England sampler saying

Bless My Family

Jesus,
Bless my family
and keep them in your sight.
If you help us all to get along,
I know we'll be all right.

My Grandparents

My grandma is so good to me,
I love her lots and lots.
She reads me tons of neat stuff
And sits with me and talks.

I love my grandpa, too, dear God.
He has the coolest way
Of teaching me to do things
And knowing what to say.

My Pet

Dear Lord,
I know my pet's not quite a person
And you've got so much to do,
But if you have a minute, God,
Could you bless my furry friend, too?

We Could Use Your Help!

Dear Jesus,
Please help my family
during this tough time.
Things aren't going too well for us,
and we could sure use your
help and guidance to get
through our problems!

My Parents

Sometimes I get confused
and wish for things
back like they were.
Sometimes I'm mad at him.
Sometimes I'm mad at her.
But I know my folks are trying,
and they love me from their hearts.
They want me to be happy,
even if they're apart.

I'm Praying for My Mother

God,
I'm praying for my mother
Who is so sick today.
I'll try to make things easy,
And help in every way.

She really needs your help, God,
A healing touch from you,
To make her feel all better
As if she were brand new.

The Bible says to ask you
And to believe with all my heart
That you will do what's best for her—
I'll trust you from the start.

Grandma and Grandpa

I'm glad you gave me such cool grandparents. I love to do things with them. They take me to the museum and the zoo. Sometimes we go on picnics or go fishing.

My grandma and grandpa like to travel, but they always hurry back because they miss us. Please bless my grandma and grandpa and keep them healthy. We sure do love each other a lot.

Be with Mom

Please be with my mom at home and at her office. She works hard in both places. Please help her get all of her work done so she can relax and have fun sometimes. I like to see her laugh and smile.

As I Grow Bigger

I know that as I grow bigger
my love for my mother and father
will grow bigger, too.
Thank you, Jesus, for my parents.

My Dad

Dear Lord, thank you for my dad.
He can do just about
anything, I think.
He carries me to bed
when I'm tired,
and he reads to me, too.
Sometimes we play ball
or cook dinner together.
You're my father, too, God,
helping me from heaven.
I'm happy I have another one
right here on Earth.
Amen.

Sister Dear

Dear Jesus,

Thank you for my sister. She likes to play the same games I do. She likes to climb our favorite tree, and she takes turns on the swing—sometimes she lets me swing longer! She is the greatest! Thank you. Amen.

Please Bless My Family

Thank you, Lord, for loving me
And all my family, too.
We know that what we have
Has been a gift from you.

Please bless my aunts and uncles
And grandparents near and far,
And don't forget my cousins, God,
You know just where they are.

Keep us safe and healthy, please,
And guard us all night through.
Thank you, Lord, for loving me
And all my family, too.
Amen.

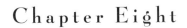

Chapter Eight

Schooltime and Playtime

As you grow older, you spend
a lot of time with friends and at school.
God wants you to have good friends
and do a good job at school.
He is interested in every area of
your life. And if you need his help,
he will be there when you talk to
him in prayer.

In all the work you are doing,
work the best you can.

—Colossians 3:23

A Friend Is Someone . . .

A friend is someone you can trust,
 even with a very important secret.
A friend will always be there,
 even when times are tough.
A friend will play your favorite game,
 even if it isn't her favorite.
A friend forgives you when you're wrong
 and still loves you in the end.
A friend is someone truly special,
 just like you, Lord Jesus Christ.

Thank You for My Teacher, God

Thank you for my teacher.
She's kind and sweet and good,
Always trying to help me
To do the things I should.

School Library

Our school library has lots of books,
God. My favorites are the ones with
lots of pictures. You must like books
as well as I do, Lord. You made so
many of them. I'm thankful for books.
They help my mind grow.

Acting Silly

Jesus, did you ever act silly when you were a little kid? My friend and I like to do funny things like make faces and tell silly jokes. We laugh and giggle a ton. It's lots of fun! Thank you for the good times we have together. I know that you are always there, laughing along with us.

I'm Trying, Lord

I'm trying, Lord
to follow the rules—
I'm trying,
you can see!

I'm trying, but sometimes
it's hard—
and the teacher gets mad at me.

I like to chat
and talk in class,
I do like to have some fun.

But I'm learning, Lord,
to do my work
and talk when school is done!

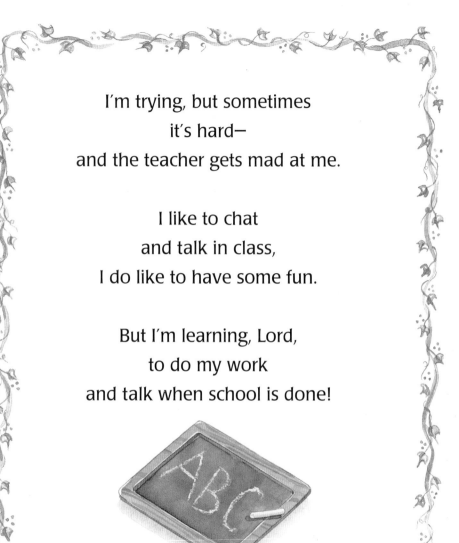

Art Class

Dear God,

Art class is my favorite class in school. I like to use paints and chalk and colored markers. Making something beautiful feels good. My grandma likes to hang my pictures on the wall. That makes me feel special. Thank you for the happy times you give me in art class. Maybe I'll be an artist someday.

Friends

Thank you for my friend next door,
And my friend across the street,
And please help me to be a friend
To everyone I meet.

—Anonymous

A Blessing from Above

Friendship always shines on a cloudy day,
Sending rainbows to guide your way.
Bright colors of joy painted with love,
A friend is a blessing from above.

Schoolwork

Dear God, I need help with my homework. When I am here alone in my room, I can't remember what the teacher said. Mom is very busy now, and Dad isn't home. Help me to remember exactly what I'm supposed to do. Thanks, God. Amen.

My Friend at School

Thank you for my friend at school. Our desks are right next to each other so we color our projects with the same colors. We eat lunch together, too. We are best friends. Thank you for giving me a friend who likes the same stuff I do. Amen.

I've Got So Much

The Lord has been so good to me,
I really feel I'm blessed.
My school is fun—I love it!
My friends are just the best!

The Lord has been so good to me,
I'm not sure what to do.
Guess I'd better thank you, God,
before this day is through!

I Like Having Friends

I have lots of friends to play with at school.
I like having friends. It's more fun to play
with someone than to play alone.

Thank you for being my friend, too, Lord.
Show me how to be a good friend to others.

I'm Okay Now

I wasn't very happy
When I had to go to school.
I didn't want to be away
And follow all those rules.

But now I've gotten used to it,
And I think it's great!
So thank you, Lord, for school.
(Just help me not be late!)

Doing My Best

Dear Jesus,

My mom says I should always do my best at school because you expect me to. When something's hard to learn I tell myself that you will help me. Then I can do it because you give me strength. Thank you for helping me like that. I know that with you, I can do anything…even if it's hard at first!

Thank You for My Friends, God

Thank you for my friends at school,
we play and have such fun—
soccer, tag, capture the flag,
or sometimes we just skip and run.

I Feel Lonely

I feel lonely today, Jesus. Everyone else seems to have friends, but I don't. Help me to know that you, Jesus Christ, are a friend to everyone and that you are the best friend I could ever hope for. With you by my side, I know that I am never truly alone.

Getting Along

Jesus,
Please help me and my friends
get along today,
so that we have lots of fun
the whole time we play!

My Friend

My friend is not too happy.
There's something that's not right.
So please, dear Lord, do what you can
To send her down your light!

My Best Friend

Thank you for my best friend, God. We are in the same class at school. We play together at recess and have so much fun! Thank you for being with us and for helping us to have such a good time.

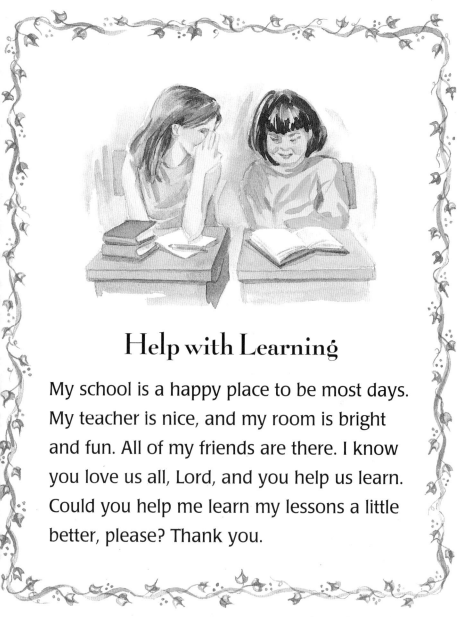

Help with Learning

My school is a happy place to be most days.
My teacher is nice, and my room is bright
and fun. All of my friends are there. I know
you love us all, Lord, and you help us learn.
Could you help me learn my lessons a little
better, please? Thank you.

A Better Kid

Please forgive me
for breaking a rule
and getting myself
into trouble at school.

I knew better,
God, I really did.
Please help me become
a much better kid.

Learning to Read

Learning to read is so cool, God! I like the stories, and I like being able to use my brain. It makes me feel smart. Thank you for giving me eyes and brains so I can enjoy reading, and thank you for so many great books.

Chosen Last

Nobody wants me on their team when we play games. I'm not very good. It doesn't feel good to be chosen last. Please help me to get better, Lord, so I can have fun with my friends. And if I do get better, please help me to remember how much it hurts others when you choose them last because they're not good. I don't ever want someone else to feel this bad!

The Kids at School

The kids at school are mean to me.
It makes me really sad.
Please help me to be friends with them,
Then I won't feel so bad.

Help Me Be a Friend, God

Dear God, protect me as I go to school. Be
my friend, and help me be a friend to others.
Amen.

My Friend Is in a Wheelchair

Dear God, my friend is in a wheelchair. It's hard for her to get around at school. People just ignore her and sometimes won't even hold the door for her. Show me how I can help her. I know she's special to you, God. She's special to me, too. Amen.

Bless My Teacher

Please bless my teacher,
Who works so hard each day.
And please bless everyone at school
For this, dear Lord, I pray.

We try so hard to learn our lessons
And the teachers do their best,
But sometimes we're not perfect, Lord,
And we put them to the test.

So, Lord, please bless my teacher,
Who works so hard at school
And help us all to help ourselves
To live the golden rule.

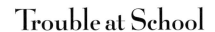

Trouble at School

There's this kid at school, God. He doesn't like me, and I don't really like him either. He tries to get me in trouble with the teacher, but I just try to ignore him. I know you wouldn't want me to be mean back to him. Help me be kind to him even if we can't be friends. Amen.

Send a Friend

Lord, I am lonely today. Everyone I know is playing with someone else. I need a special friend to play with and share with and be happy with. Please send me a friend.

To See Me Through

God, is it okay to ask you for help with school? I pay attention and try really hard, but sometimes I think I could use an extra little prayer to see me through! Please help me to understand my schoolwork and make me patient when I'm having trouble with it. Amen.

We're Lucky to Have School

When I get frustrated
and think staying home
would be so neat,
I try to think of kids
who don't have school
and don't get enough to eat.

I know I am so lucky
to have the things I do.
I'll try not to complain
and remember to thank you!

Field Trips

Dear God,

My class field trip was so much fun. My friends and I got to see all kinds of new things! I love that there is always so much new stuff for me to learn. Thank you for giving us such a big, wide world to explore. It's great!

My Friend Is Hurt

My friend broke his leg and can't come to school. Can you make him feel better, Lord? Please don't let his leg hurt very much. Help him to heal so he can come back to school soon, and we can run around together again.

You're My Friend, Lord

I've got friends at home
and I've got friends at school—
but you, Lord, are my best friend
and I think that's so cool!

Blessed with Friends

You've blessed me
with so many friends
that all my fun
will never end!

Playing with My Friend

I had a good time with my friend today, God. It's fun playing together. We make each other happy. I'm glad you created friends, Lord. Life is a lot more fun when you can share it with nice and caring people!

Chapter Nine

All Creatures Great & Small

Sometimes we don't know what to say when we pray. We think our words sound silly. But God created *all* words, and no word is strange to him. We can thank him for everything in the world because he made it all! We can ask him for help—he knows the answer to every situation. He is a very wise God.

Through his power all things were made—things in heaven and on earth.

—Colossians 1:16

Wow!

I looked around today,
And you know what I found?
I saw a million miracles
Just waiting all around!

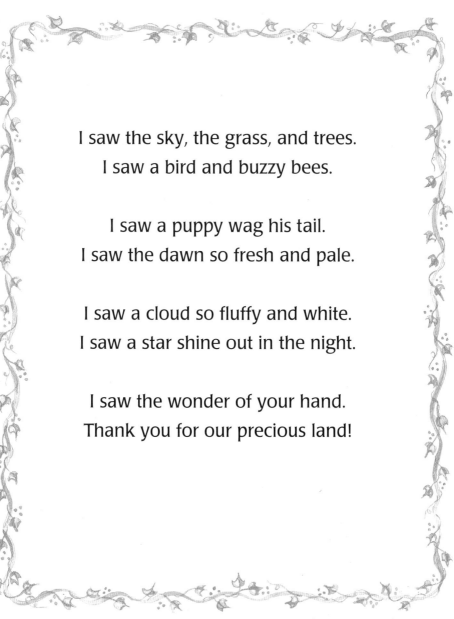

I saw the sky, the grass, and trees.
I saw a bird and buzzy bees.

I saw a puppy wag his tail.
I saw the dawn so fresh and pale.

I saw a cloud so fluffy and white.
I saw a star shine out in the night.

I saw the wonder of your hand.
Thank you for our precious land!

Thank You for the Sun

Thank you for the sun in the morning
and the moon that shines at night.

Thank you for my family
and everyone who loves me.

Thank you for this good, green earth
and for my special life.

The Wind Tells Me

The wind tells me,
The birds tell me,
The Bible tells me, too,
How much our Father loves us all,
And now I'm telling you.

I Believe...

Dear God,
I believe in wishing
and rainbows
and dreams coming true—
I believe in all
of those things,
'cause I believe in YOU!

Ants

Lord, I really like ants. They are like little people. They always work to carry things like food and leaves. They are pretty smart, too. They live in big families so nobody gets lonely. I think that sounds like a nice life. Thanks for making ants. Amen.

Our Country's Beauty

We thank you, Father,

For blue lakes that sparkle in the sun,

For green forests that reach to touch the sky,

For purple mountains that poke their heads
through clouds,

For yellow fields of grain that wave to the
passing wind.

We thank you, Father, for the beauty of our
country.

This Land

I am so proud
to be a part
of this beautiful country—
to know the blessings
we enjoy every day.
And I pray for a time
when everyone
is happy and fed
and all the people
in our wonderful land—
no matter what they believe
or the color of their skin—
may live in peace.

Amen.

I Love to Sit Outside

I love to sit outside
and see
all the cool things that fly
by me.

Butterflies, birds,
and buzzing bees.
I smell the flowers
and feel the breeze.

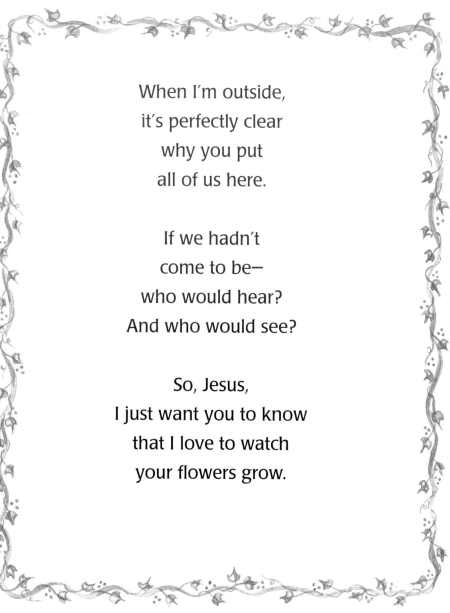

When I'm outside,
it's perfectly clear
why you put
all of us here.

If we hadn't
come to be—
who would hear?
And who would see?

So, Jesus,
I just want you to know
that I love to watch
your flowers grow.

Butterflies

Dear God,

Thank you for butterflies. They are so pretty.
When they fly, they seem so free. I would
like to be free and fly anywhere I want to go.
I could see lots of neat stuff. I could fly high
up in the treetops and look into a bird's nest.
I could fly from garden to garden and check
out all the beautiful flowers.

You've Sure Been Busy!

I don't know how you did it,
But you sure did it right.
Mountains, fields, and oceans—
And then there's day and night!

I don't know why it happened
That you would put us here.
I only know it's obvious
That you are always near!

Rainbows Are Cool!

Red
is for the love you give.

Orange
is bright and fun.

Yellow
stands for the sunshine
that shines on everyone!

Green
is all things growing.

Blue
is for the sea.

And *Purple*
is just plain silly.
(It's a lot like me!)

Thank you for
the rainbow.
Thank you for
the light.
Thank you, God,
for everything.
You made it all
just right!

For This Good Land

Thank you, Lord,
for this good, green land—
everywhere I look,
I see your hand.

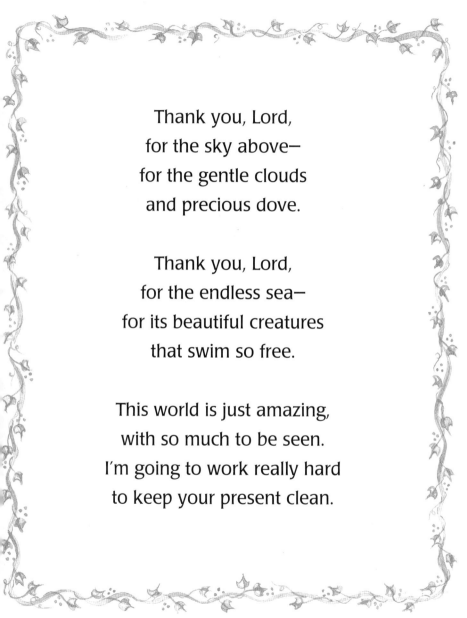

Thank you, Lord,
for the sky above—
for the gentle clouds
and precious dove.

Thank you, Lord,
for the endless sea—
for its beautiful creatures
that swim so free.

This world is just amazing,
with so much to be seen.
I'm going to work really hard
to keep your present clean.

Out in Space

I looked out at the stars one night
and found myself in awe.
There were so many twinkling lights
and planets that I saw.

The solar system is so wide,
and we are just a part
of this great big universe
you keep within your heart.

I wonder, God, at nighttime
as I look up at the sky
if any other kids look up,
and ask the same thing: Why?

Thank You for Your Creation

Thank you for the sunshine,
Thank you for the rain,
Thank you for the birds on high
Who sing their sweet refrain.

Thank you for the mountains
So beautiful to see.
Thank you for the tall, green grass
That tickles at my feet.

Thank you for creation,
All that you have made—
Each tree, each plant and flower
So wonderfully displayed.

Hurt No Living Thing

Hurt no living thing:
Ladybird, nor butterfly,
Nor moth with dusty wing,
Nor cricket chirping cheerily,
Nor grasshopper so light of leap,
Nor dancing gnat, nor beetle fat,
Nor harmless worms that creep.

—Christina Rossetti

Thanks for Bugs and Worms

God, thanks for making bugs and worms. I love them. They are so interesting to watch. They have so many colors and so many neat designs! Thanks, God—you really know what kids like. Amen.

What Makes the Grass Grow?

What makes grass grow, I wonder,
What makes the sky so blue?
I think I know the answer, Lord,
I know it's all from YOU!

The Sunset

I love to see a sunset
With pink, yellow, and blue.
It seems a perfect ending
To a day with much to do.

Thanks, God, for the sunset.
When I see one then I know
That you must surely love me
To give me such a show.

Thank You for the Flowers

God, flowers are so pretty. I love to smell them. Each petal looks perfect and feels so soft. Their bright colors make me feel so happy! Thank you for the flowers, God. You sure can make some pretty things! Amen.

Clouds

I love to look up in the sky
and watch the passing clouds.
They look so soft and beautiful,
it makes my heart say, "Wow!"

Do you use them for a pillow—
a place to lay your head?
I would like to try a few
to throw upon my bed.

Thank you, God, for clouds.

I Like Mud

I like mud, God. It squishes through my toes. It feels cool on my hands when I try to make things with it. Then when it rains again, all the stuff I made gets flattened down again. That is *so* amazing, God. The rain you send has so much power. Thanks for mud.

Planet Home

This home of ours
is pretty cool, Lord—
with all the animals
and people and
beautiful land.

I know that sometimes
we don't
take care of it
the way you would like.

I think we're trying
to do a better job.
I hope to help with that
even more as I grow up.

We have such an incredible
home that we've just GOT
to take care of it.

You can count on me
to help clean it up, Lord.
I want to be sure
we keep your gift
to us special.

How Did You Make the World?

God, how did you make the world? Did you roll the earth in your hands to make it round? I like the way you painted it all those beautiful colors. I like to make pretty things, too, God. Since you are my heavenly father, I guess I must have gotten that from you! Thanks. Amen.

Thank You for the World

Thank you for the mountains,
Thank you for the sea,
Thank you for the tall trees
That bring some shade to me.

Thank you for the glowing sun
And for the moon at night.
Thank you for each twinkling star
That shines so nice and bright.

Thank you, God, for everything
You made to give us joy—
Each animal and flower,
Each girl and every boy.

Let's Look at the World Together

My world is small, God, and I only really know my neighborhood. I wonder what other places are like.

It must be neat to sit in heaven and look at all of the beautiful places that you have made. Someday I'm going to sit right next to you and finally get to see them all. That will be great! Amen.

Thank You, God, for Birds

Birds in the treetops,
Birds on the fence,
Birds singing in my yard
And even on our bench.

Always bringing joy and love
To everyone who hears
The pretty songs God gave them
To bring us all some cheer.

Thank you, God, for all these birds
Who share their notes so sweet.
It fills my heart with joy and love
To hear their *tweet, tweet, tweet.*

Rainy Days

I like sunny days, but rain is good, too. It washes the streets and makes them clean. Rain makes plants grow and gives us water to drink. We can't live without water, so I'm glad we have rain sometimes. Thank you, Lord. You give us what we need.

Save the Earth

Dear God,
You created the earth
and gave it to us to care for.
Teach us how to save the land,
to keep our air and oceans clean,
to be careful how we use your gifts
of water, wildlife, and forests
so they will last forever.

Cloud Show

Today the clouds are a fuzzy, white blanket
spread across the sky.
Yesterday there were castles and mountains
and creatures floating by.

What surprises will come tomorrow, Lord?
What wonders will there be?
Thank you for the cloud show
that you put on just for me.

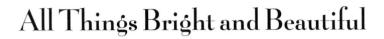

All Things Bright and Beautiful

All things bright and beautiful,
All creatures great and small,
All things wise and wonderful:
The Lord God made them all.

Each little flower that opens,
Each little bird that sings,
God made their glowing colors,
And made their tiny wings.

—Cecil Frances Alexander

A Bird Concert

Dear God, today I heard a bird singing,
and I stopped to listen.
It was dressed in bright red from head to toe.
It gave a concert just for me.
Thank you, God,
For happy birdsongs.

For the Beauty of the Earth

For the beauty of the earth,
For the glory of the skies,
For the love which from our birth
Over and around us lies,
Lord of all, to you we raise
This our hymn of grateful praise.

For the wonder of each hour
Of the day and of the night,
Hill and vale and tree and flower,
Sun and moon, and stars of light:
Lord of all, to you we raise
This our hymn of grateful praise.

—Folliott Sandford Pierpoint

Chapter Ten

Special Prayers for Special Days

Many of the special days we have are given to us because God loves us. Christmas is Jesus' birthday. Easter is for celebrating new life. Mother's Day and Father's Day are to honor our parents, and Valentine's Day is for showing love to others. Thank God for all your special times.

Enjoy serving the Lord.

—Psalm 37:4

Happy Birthday to Me

Dear God, today is my birthday. It is my very own holiday to celebrate the day I was born. Thank you for making me and for giving me parents who love me. Thank you for my friends and family, who help make my day special. Thank you for birthday cakes and parties and presents and lots of fun. Happy birthday to me!

Holiday Dinner

For the holidays, when families get together,
 We thank you, Lord.
For the feast prepared by many hands,
 We thank you, Lord.
For the good times shared around the table,
 We thank you, Lord.
For the family encircled by your love,
 We thank you, Lord.

The Seasons

Thank you for the springtime
when the flowers start to grow.
All the birds sing happy songs,
and the green grass starts to show.

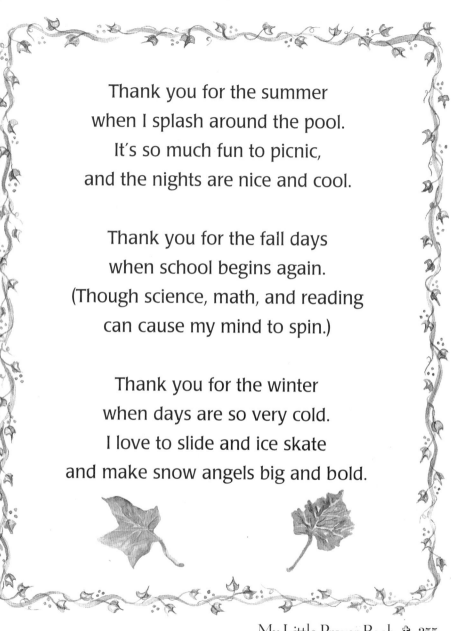

Thank you for the summer
when I splash around the pool.
It's so much fun to picnic,
and the nights are nice and cool.

Thank you for the fall days
when school begins again.
(Though science, math, and reading
can cause my mind to spin.)

Thank you for the winter
when days are so very cold.
I love to slide and ice skate
and make snow angels big and bold.

A New Year

Dear God,

It's fun to say hello to the new year and blow horns and throw paper streamers in the air. It's like a birthday party for the world. Thank you for this brand-new year. You help us start all over again. Now we can try to do things better.

Martin Luther King Jr. Day

I know you don't care what color a person's skin is. You love everyone no matter what they look like. Thank you for sending Dr. Martin Luther King Jr. so the world could learn that, too. That's pretty cool, God. When I grow up, I want to teach people your important lessons like Dr. King did.

Valentine's Party

I love to give valentines
to the friends at school I meet.
We celebrate, have some fun,
and then we have a treat.

When I give cards to my friends,
it's like I'm doing my part
to show each and every one
how much they're in your heart!

Presidents' Day

Dear God,

Bless our president today. Please help him to be a strong leader. Thank you for George Washington and Abraham Lincoln and all the other presidents who have helped our country grow.

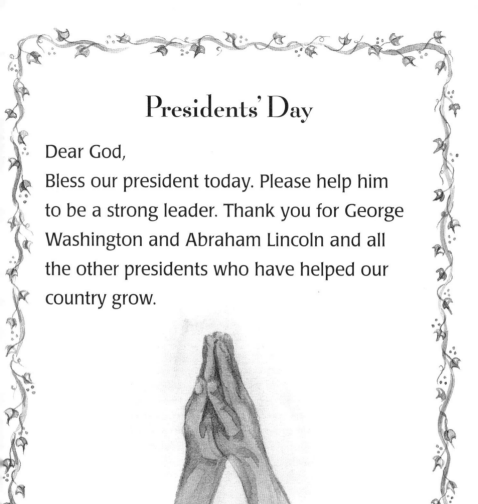

Saint Patrick's Day

I like to think I'm Irish
On this day for wearing green,
But shamrocks and leprechauns
Are not what this day means.

It's all about Saint Patrick
Who to his world did give
The message of the gospel
So his countrypeople could live.

Thank you for Saint Patrick, God.

Eastertime

This is a special time of year,
When spring is in the air
And all our thoughts turn to you, Lord,
Remembering how much you care.
For you were born and died for us,
Sent from the Father above.
And so at Easter, Jesus,
I send you all my love.

I Love Easter

God,
I like to think of Easter
Because of your great Son,
Who died because he loved me
And brought hope to everyone.
Amen.

Easter Sunday

Dear Jesus,
Good Friday was sad
Because you died on a cross.
But Easter Sunday you
 came alive again.
You took away our old
 lives and gave us
 new ones.
Thank you
 for that.

Earth Day Prayer

We thank you for the earth today,
The trees, the plants and flowers.
You painted everything just right
To bring us all the colors.

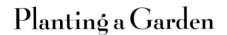

Planting a Garden

Dear God,

The earth is waking, there's no more snow,

We have holes to dig and seeds to sow.

We'll plant the seeds

And pull the weeds

And water up and down the row.

So you, dear Lord, can help our garden grow.

Mother's Day Prayer

I don't know how she does it, God,
but she sure does do it well.
And I don't know how to say it, God—
my love is so hard to tell.
Please help me to show it to her
so Mom will know for sure
that I'm really, truly, absolutely
filled with love for her!
Please bless my
mom today,
God. It's her
special day.
Amen.

Spring Is a Celebration

Spring is a celebration, when all the earth wakes up from a winter's nap. Tiny blades of grass reach for the sun. Trees sprout leaves. Buds and flowers come out of the ground. Birds build nests. The whole world smells sweet. Thank you, God, for spring.

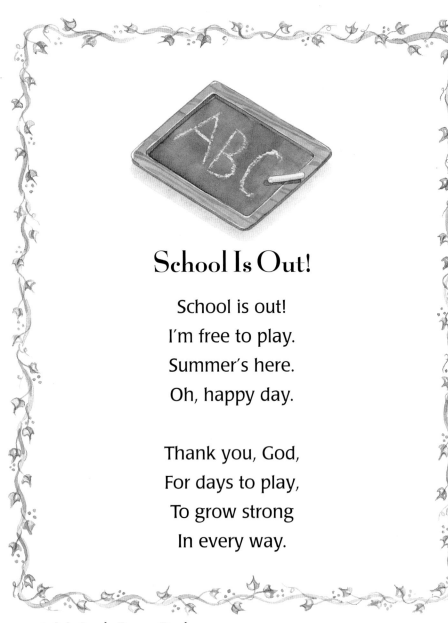

School Is Out!

School is out!
I'm free to play.
Summer's here.
Oh, happy day.

Thank you, God,
For days to play,
To grow strong
In every way.

Summer Vacation

School's out for the summer,
no more work to do!
School's out for the summer,
it's finally come true!

When school's out for the summer
and we play in the sun's heat,
It gives me a special feeling
that just cannot be beat!

And I'm so very thankful
when summertime is here,
To spend my happy summer
with the friends whom I hold dear!

Father's Day Prayer

My dad sure deserves
a special day.
I pray that he is blessed.
My dad is such a special guy—
as dads go, he's the best!

Summer

Summer is dressed in a green velvet gown
   with splashes of flowery colors around.
Summer's alive with grasses and trees
   with spiders and birds, mosquitoes and
   bees.
God, you make my summer a time for fun.
   I'm kissed by the breeze and hugged by
   the sun.

The Sunshine

When the days are
warm and happy,
and the sunshine
lands on me,
I am such a happy kid—
you'd be so proud of me!

I Start School Tomorrow

Dear God,

It is the first day of school tomorrow. I'm excited, but I feel nervous, too. Will I like my new teacher? Can I find my new room? Will I be able to do all the things I should? Be with me, Lord. Help me feel calm. With you beside me, I can do anything.

First Day of School

Dear God,
I have a big day today.
It is my first day at school.
Please help me to be strong
and not miss my family too much.
Help me to be kind to everyone
I meet, even if they don't smile
at me first. Guide me as I cross
the street, and help me
keep my new shoes clean.
Thank you, God. I will try to learn
as much as I can.
Amen.

Autumn

Orange, gold, and brown—
Autumn leaves are falling down.
Yellow, green, and red—
God will put the earth to bed.
Summer's gone away—
Winter soon will come to stay.

Crispy, Crunchy, Crackly Fall

I rake the yard
and walk in leaves.
They go
> *crunch!*
> *snap!*
> *crackle!*

I go inside for hot chocolate
by the fireplace.
The fire goes
> *pop!*
> *sizzle!*
> *crack!*

Thank you, God, for noisy fall days.

Silly, Spooky Time

Tonight I'll wear my costume
and go to trick or treat.
I'll have fun with my friends
and get a lot of sweets.

It's cool to dress up with my friends
and look silly for a day.
I pray for a Halloween
that's safe in every way!

Veterans Day Prayer

Thank you for our heroes,
The brave, the tough, the strong,
Who died for our great nation
With freedom as their song.

Thanksgiving

Dear God,
Thanksgiving time is filled with prayers
And food, fun, and good cheer.
But we should thank you, loving God,
Every day of the whole year.

Thanksgiving Dinner

We thank you for the food we eat,
We thank you for our health,
We thank you for this land of ours
That's filled with so much wealth,
So thank you, God, for everything
That's good and true and right.
Please bless us, God, forever
And keep us in your sight!

Winter

Dear Lord,
Thank you for winter,
when the earth sleeps
in the cold air
and has a bright
blanket of snow
covering her.

Winter Fun

Dear God, thank you
for the fun of winter—
for sledding,
sliding,
skating,
skiing,
and snow!
You show us your love in every season.

The Christmas Season

It's almost your birthday, Jesus!
We've put up our pretty tree,
and I want to share with you
just what it means to me.

Now presents are sure fun to get,
I won't deny that's true.
But there's something more important
that I want to say to you.

'Cause Christmas isn't about the gifts,
though giving plays a part.
What's really, truly important
is what's inside our hearts.

Christmas Reminder

Christmas is the time of year
We like to think of friends.
Giving gifts and presents,
It never seems to end.

I love each Christmas season
With lights, good food, and tree.
I won't forget the meaning, though,
Jesus came to Earth for me!

Thank you, God, for Christmas.

Christmas Day

Dear God,
On this day, long ago,
You gave us Jesus
To be our Savior.
No wonder the angels sang!